40 HADITH ON
WEALTH AND EARNING

أَرْبَعُوْنَ حَدِيْثًا فِي الْمَالِ وَالتَّكَسُّبِ

By Joe W. Bradford

The cover image is a derivative of "Ya'qub al-Layth's Silver Dirham", by CoinArchives, licensed under Creative Commons Attribution 4.0 international, Modified from original.

(URL: https://commons.wikimedia.org/wiki/File:Ya%27qub_al-Layth%27s_Silver_Dirham_2.jpg, last accessed 29NOV22)

Printed in the United States of America

2nd Print, 1st Edition, 2022.

ISBN 978-0-9965192-5-0

Origem Publishing

www.OrigemPublishing.com

Table of Contents

فهرس المحتويات

ix

Foreword

In the name of Allah, the Beneficent, the Merciful

All praise is due, with praise of the grateful, and I send blessings and peace upon the master of the first and last generations, Muhammad who was sent as a mercy to all worlds, on upon his illustrious family and companions, and all those that follow their guidance and walks in their footsteps until the Day of Reckoning.

To proceed: The scholars of this Umma produced a variety of works to preserve the Hadith. From the most famous of these hadith works is the Forty Hadith genre, the first person having written a collection of 40 hadith – as mentioned explicitly by Abu Tahir al-Silafi – was al-Imam Abdullah ibn al-Mubarak (died 181h), of which seventeen hadith were printed. Following these footsteps our scholars – may Allah be pleased with them – authored innumerable works in this genre, reworking how they presented this material and its contents with regards to both Hadith texts and their chains.

In this vein we have this enjoyable hadith collection entitled "Forty Hadith on Wealth and Earning" by our brother, the industrious Sheikh Joe Bradford, trailing the path set by our Hadith masters, in transmitting the Sunnah of the Prophet (K), in calling for it to be acted upon, and in seeking blessings through abundant prayers for the intercessor of creation, the master of the first and last generations, may Allah's prayers and peace be upon him.

He expertly chose what to include in this collection, the best of which being the variety of hadith he included, those related to contract law, as well ethical, financial, and behavioral hadith. He enhanced this selection by accompanying each hadith a definitivee

Quranic verse or an established jurisprudential maxim, and at times even establishing an Islamic financial concept in order to refute an incorrect western one. He then embellished this presentation by translating it into English, so its benefit extends to both Arabs and non-Arabs.

In conclusion, I ask Allah – Mighty and High – to bless the one who collected it, to benefit its reader, and to forgive the one who wrote this foreword.

And the last of our prayers is that all praise is due to Allah, Lord of the worlds.

Written by:

Abdulkader Amor Al Idrisi

تقديم

الحمد لله حمد الشاكرين، وأصلي وأسلم على سيد الأولين والآخرين، محمد المبعوث رحمة للعالمين، وعلى آله وصحبه الغر الميامين، ومن اتبع هديهم واقتفى أثرهم إلى يوم الدين.

وبعد: فقد تفنن علماء الأمة في حفظ الحديث والتأليف فيه، ومن أشهر أصناف الكتب الحديثية الأربعينات، وأول من صنَّف فيها كما صرح أبو طاهر السِّلَفي: الإمام عبدالله بن المبارك (ت 181هـ)[1]. وطبع منها 17 حديثا[2]. ثم صنَّف العلماء – رضي الله عنهم – في هذا الباب ما لا يُحصَى من المصنَّفات[3]. وتفننوا في طرائقها ومضامينها؛ متنا وإسنادا.

---

[1] – الأربعون البلدانية (ص17).

[2] – طبع ضمن كتاب «الإمام عبدالله بن المبارك المروزي، المحدث الناقد»، للدكتور: محمد سعيد بخاري (ص186 – 200).

[3] – مقدمة الأربعين للإمام النووي (ص39 – 42).

ويأتي هذه الجزء الحديثي الماتع الموسوم بـ: الأربعين حديثا في المال والتكسب، لأخينا الشيخ الهُمام جو برادفورد. متأسيا بسادتنا المحدثين، في التبليغ لسنة النبي ﷺ، والدعوة للعمل بها، والتبرك بكثرة الصلاة على شفيع الخلق وسيد الأولين والآخرين ﷺ.

وقد أحسن أيما إحسان في جمعها، ولعل من أفضل ذلك تنوع الأحاديث بين أبواب الفقه في الدين؛ من أحاديث عقدية مالية، وفقهية وسلوكية وأخلاقية. وقد زانها بربطها بآية محكمة أو قاعدة فقهية معتمدة. أو حتى تأصيل لمفهوم مالي إسلامي؛ ورد على مفهوم غربي خاطئ. ثم وشَّحها بترجمتها بالإنجليزية ليعم النفع بها عربا وعجما.

وأخيرا أسأل الله عزوجل أن يبارك في جامعها، وينفع قارئها ويغفر لمقدمها.

وآخر دعوانا إن الحمد لله رب العالمين.

كتبه:

عبد القادر عمور الإدريسي

XV

Introduction

In the name of Allah, the Beneficent, the Merciful

All praise is due to Allah, Lord of the Worlds, and may He send peace and blessing upon the one He dispatched as a mercy to all worlds, our prophet Muḥammad, his family, companions, and all who follow them in righteousness until the Day of Reckoning.

Throughout Islamic history numerous scholars have composed collections of forty hadith. Perhaps the most well-known of them being the Forty Hadith of al-Imām al-Nawawī (d. 676H), while one of the earliest was collected by Al-Hasan b. Sufyan Al-Nasawi (d. 303H), a student of Imam Ahmad b. Hanbal. Numerous other scholars throughout the ages have compiled forty hadith collections on a plethora of topics: some on faith, some on Jihād, others on Zuhd, and still others on topics related to Fiqh.

The notion that inspired this book came from my many conversations with Sh. AbdulKader Amor, a unique thinker in the area of Islamic finance whom I've spent hours upon hours with discussing issues of Fiqh, Usool, Hadith, and issues of business and finance specially. He would often draw my attention to hadith related to financial and business ethics that were broader is perspective than being related only to actionable Islamic legal minutiae.

So I sought Allah's counsel on compiling 40 hadith – as al-Imām al-Nawawī before me said – seeking to follow "...in the footsteps of the aforementioned notable scholars and hadith masters of Islam." The goal of this text is to mention the fundamental texts through which concepts vital to the study of wealth, earning, economics, finance, and financial ethics, will be introduced from an Islamic lens.

In mentioning the texts, I attributed each hadith to its source, deleted its chain of narrations except for the Companion who narrated the hadith. The grading of narrations outside of the two Sahihs are mentioned from the statements of the Imams of Hadith. Several hadith are accompanied by pithy explanations of important terms. Each hadith is preceded by a chapter heading which is either a related verse of the Quran or a maxim related to the meaning of the hadith. My immense gratitude goes out to all those that helped review this work, especially Abdullah al-Rabbat, Abdullah Moataz, and Deniza Mustafic.

I've named it "Forty Hadith on Wealth and Earning" and I ask Allah to make it beneficial.

Joe Bradford

بِسْمِ ٱللهِ ٱلرَّحْمَنِ ٱلرَّحِيمِ

الحمد لله رب العاملين والصلاة والسلام على المبعوث رحمة للعاملين نبينا محمد وعلى اله واصحابه ومن اتبعهم برضوان الى يوم الدين. وبعد :

فقد صنف علماء الإسلام على مر التاريخ — مصنفات جمعوا فيها أربعين حديثا. فمن أشهرهم الإمام يحيى بن شرف النووي، ومن أقدمهم الحسن بن سفيان النسوي المتوفى سنة 303هـ، من تلاميذ الإمام أحمد بن حنبل إلى غيرهما عبر القرون من العلماء ممن جمعوا أربعينات في أبواب الإسلام المختلفة ، من الإيمان، والجهاد ، والزهد، والفقه إلى غير ذلك.

والفكرة الملهمة لهذا الكتاب جاءت أثناء محادثاتي العديدة مع الشيخ عبد القادر عمور الإدريسي ، وهو مفكر فريد من نوعه في مجال التمويل الإسلامي فقد قضيت الساعات الطوال معه لمدراسة ومناقشة قضايا الفقه والأصول والحديث وبخاصة قضايا التمويل والعمل ، حيث كان يشير أحيانا إلى أحاديث ذات صلة بأخلاقيات التمويل والعمل مما له مدرك أوسع من مجرد الفرع الفقهي الجزئي العملي.

فاستخرت الله تعالى في جمع أربعين حديثا – كما قال الامام النووي قبلي – اقتداءً بالأئمة الأعلام وحفّاظ الإسلام ، بهدف ذكر نصوص الأحاديث التي تنبني عليها مفاهيم المال والكسب والاقتصاد والتمويل والأخلاقيات المالية من منظور الشرع.

واعتمدت فيه عزو كل حديث إلى مصدره من الكتب المسندة ، مع حذف أسانيدها عدا راوي الحديث، وما كان في الصحيحين أو أحدهما اكتفيت به ، وأما الأحاديث في غيرهما فذكرت كلام أئمة الحديث عليها. وبعض الأحاديث مصحوبة بشرح مختصر لبعض الألفاظ المهمة فيها. وبوّبت كل حديث بما يتعلق به من آيات كتاب الله أو القواعد الفقهية و المالية ذات الصلة. وأقدم الشكر الجزيل لجميع من ساعد في مراجعة هذا العمل، وأخص بالذكر هنا عبد الله الرباط وعبد الله معتز ودنيزا مصطفى.

وسميته «أربعين حديثا في المال والتكسب» سائلا المولى جل جلاله أن ينفع به.

وكتبه : أبو لقمان هود جو برادفورد

Hadith 1

In contracts, consideration is given to objectives and meanings

Al-Bukhārī collects from 'Umar: Allah's messenger ﷺ said:

"Actions are by intention, and every man will have what he intended. He who emigrates for Allah and His Messenger, then his emigration was to Allah and His Messenger. He who emigrated to earn some wealth, or to marry some woman, then his emigration was to that which he traveled to."

الحديث الأول

العبرة في العقود بالقصود والمعاني

رَوَى البخاري عَنْ عُمَرَ : أَنَّ رَسُولَ اللَّهِ ﷺ قَالَ:

«الأَعْمَالُ بِالنِّيَّةِ، وَلِكُلِّ امْرِئٍ مَا نَوَى، فَمَنْ كَانَتْ هِجْرَتُهُ إِلَى اللَّهِ وَرَسُولِهِ فَهِجْرَتُهُ إِلَى اللَّهِ وَرَسُولِهِ، وَمَنْ كَانَتْ هِجْرَتُهُ لِدُنْيَا يُصِيبُهَا، أَوِ امْرَأَةٍ يَتَزَوَّجُهَا، فَهِجْرَتُهُ إِلَى مَا هَاجَرَ إِلَيْهِ».

Hadith 2

The Most High's statement : Whoever wants the life of this world and its adornment...

Al-Tirmidhī collects from Anas who said, Allah's messenger ﷺ said:

"Whoever makes the Hereafter his concern, Allah makes his heart rich, organizes his affairs, and the world comes to him lessened and willingly[4]. And whoever makes the world his concern, Allah puts his poverty right before his eyes, and disorganizes his affairs, and the world does not come to him, except what has been decreed for him."

This narration contains Yazīd b. Abān al-Raqqāshi, who is weak; it has supporting narrations from the hadith of al-Hasan from Anas narrated by al-Bazzār, as well as from the hadith of Zaid b. Thābit in the Musnad of Ahmad. This narration was graded Sahih by al-Albāni.

---

[4] - Lessened and willingly is the transation I have chosen for (وَهِيَ رَاغِمَةٌ), based on the explanation for this phrase given by Mulla Ali Qari in Mirqat al-Mafatih "that is: lessened and humiliated, following after him; He needs not much effort to attain it. Instead, it will come to him easily and softly, despite its opposition or the opposition of its masters." See 8/3334.

الحديث الثاني

قوله تعالى : مَن كَانَ يُرِيدُ الْحَيَاةَ الدُّنْيَا وَزِينَتَها ... الآية

روى التِّرمذي عَنْ أَنَسِ بْنِ مَالِكٍ قَالَ: قَالَ رَسُولُ اللَّهِ ﷺ:

«مَنْ كَانَتِ الآخِرَةُ هَمَّهُ جَعَلَ اللَّهُ غِنَاهُ في قَلْبِهِ وَجَمَعَ لَهُ شَمْلَهُ، وَأَتَتْهُ الدُّنْيَا وَهِيَ رَاغِمَةٌ [5]، وَمَنْ كَانَتِ الدُّنْيَا هَمَّهُ جَعَلَ اللَّهُ فَقْرَهُ بَيْنَ عَيْنَيْهِ، وَفَرَّقَ عَلَيْهِ شَمْلَهُ، وَلَمْ يَأْتِهِ مِنَ الدُّنْيَا إِلَّا مَا قُدِّرَ لَهُ»

وفيه يزيد بن أبان الرقاشي وهو ضعيف، وله شواهد من حديث الحسن عن أنس رواه البزار، وآخر من حديث زيد بن ثابت عند أحمد، والحديث صححه الألباني.

---

[5] – قال القاري في مرقاة المفاتيح (أيْ: ذَلِيلَةٌ حَقِيرَةٌ تَابِعَةٌ لَهُ، لا يَحْتَاجُ في طَلَبِها إلى سَعْيٍ كَثِيرٍ، بَلْ تَأْتِيهِ هَيِّنَةً لَيِّنَةً، عَلَى رَغْمِ أَنْفِها وأَنْفِ أَرْبابِها). انظر 3334/8.

Hadith 3

Seeking dunya is like drinking alcohol, the more you drink the more you thirst.

Al-Bazzār collects from Ibn ʿAbbās in Marfu' form:

"Two that are hungry and never satisfied: a seeker of knowledge and a seeker of dunya."

Al-Hākim collects in his Mustadrak from Anas from the Prophet ﷺ with a similar wording:

"Two unsatiated that are never satisfied: one unsatiated in knowledge, he is never satisfied; and one unsatiated in Dunya, he is never satisfied."

Al-Hākim said: This is a sound hadith on the condition of the two shaikhs which they did not record; I have not found a single defect for it. Al-Dhahabi agreed.

الحديث الثالث

مثل طالب الدنيا كشارب الخمر ، كلما شرب عطش

روى البزار عن ابن عباس رفعه:

«منهومان لا يشبعان: طالب علم وطالب دنيا.»

وروى الحاكم في مستدركه عن أنس عن النبي ﷺ قوله :

« منهومان لا يشبعان : منهوم في علم لا يشبع ، ومنهوم في دنيا لا

يشبع .»

وقال الحاكم : هذا حديث صحيح على شرط الشيخين و لم يخرجاه و لم أجد له

علة. ووافقه الذهبي.

Hadith 4

The Most High's statement: There is not a creature on Earth except it is on Allah to sustain it.

Al-Tirmidhī collects from ʿUmar ibn al-Khaṭṭāb: Allah's messenger ﷺ said:

"If you would only rely on Allah in truth, you would be sustained like the birds; they leave their nests in the morning empty and return in the evening with full stomachs."

Abu Eisa al-Tirmidhi said: This is a Hasan Sahih hadith.

الحديث الرابع

قوله تعالى : وَمَا مِنْ دَابَّةٍ فِي الْأَرْضِ إِلَّا عَلَى اللَّهِ رِزْقُهَا ...الآية

روى التِّرمذي عَنْ عُمَرَ بْنِ الْخَطَّابِ قَالَ : قَالَ رَسُولُ اللَّهِ ﷺ :

« لَوْ أَنَّكُمْ كُنْتُمْ تَوَكَّلُونَ عَلَى اللَّهِ حَقَّ تَوَكُّلِهِ لَرُزِقْتُمْ كَمَا يُرْزَقُ الطَّيْرُ تَغْدُو خِمَاصًا وَتَرُوحُ بِطَانًا.»

قال أبو عيسى هذا حديث حسن صحيح.

Hadith 5

Wealth is not having lots of possessions

Al-Nasā'ī and Ibn Ḥibbān collect from Abū Dharr that the Prophet ﷺ said:

"O Abū Dharr, do you think that lots of money is wealth? Wealth is only the wealth of the heart and poverty is poverty of the heart. Whoever has wealth in his heart then nothing he faces in this life will harm him. Whoever has poverty in his heart then nothing he accumulates in this life will be enough for him. The only thing that will harm him is his miserliness."

Shaikh Shu'ayb al-Arna'ut said: This hadith is Sahih per the conditions of Muslim.

الحديث الخامس

ليس الغنى عن كثرة العرض

روى النسائي وابن حبان عن أبي ذر ﷺ : أن النبي ﷺ قال :

«يا أبا ذَرٍّ ! أتَرَى أنَّ كثرةَ المالِ هو الغِنَى ؟ إنما الغِنَى غِنَى القلبِ ، والفقرُ فقرُ القلبِ، مَن كان الغِنَى في قلبِه ، فلا يَضُرُّه ما لَقِيَ من الدنيا ، ومَن كان الفقرُ في قلبِه ، فلا يُغْنِيهِ ما أُكْثِرَ له في الدنيا ، وإنما يَضُرُّ نَفْسَه شُحُّها.»

قال الشيخ شعيب الأرنؤوط: إسناده صحيح على شرط مسلم.

Hadith 6

Whoever is permitted to take something, is permitted to ask for it.

Muslim collects from ʿAbdullāh from the Prophet ﷺ that he used to say:

"Lord, I ask of You guidance, piety, chastity, and wealth."

الحديث السادس

من أبيح له أخذ شيء أبيح له سؤاله

روى مسلم عَنْ عَبْدِ اللَّهِ، عَنِ النبي ﷺ أَنَّهُ كَانَ يَقُولُ:

«اللَّهُمَّ إِنِّي أَسْأَلُكَ الْهُدَى، وَالتُّقَى، وَالْعَفَافَ، وَالْغِنَى»

Hadith 7

Earning for worldly delights is permissible

Ibn Ḥibbān collects in his Sahih from Saʿad ibn Abī Waqqāṣ, who said: Allah's messenger ﷺ said:

"Four things are from happiness: A righteous wife, a spacious dwelling, a good neighbor, and a good mount. Four things are from misery: A terrible neighbor, a terrible wife, a cramped dwelling, and a terrible mount. "

الحديث السابع

الاكتساب لحظوظ الدنيا مباح

روى ابن حبان في صحيحه عن سعد بن أبي وقاص قَالَ: قَالَ رَسُولُ اللَّهِ ﷺ:

«أربعٌ مِنَ السَّعادةِ: المرأةُ الصَّالحةُ والمسكَنُ الواسعُ والجارُ الصَّالحُ والمركَبُ الهنيءُ، وأربعٌ مِنَ الشَّقاوةِ: الجارُ السَّوءُ والمرأةُ السَّوءُ والمسكَنُ الضَّيِّقُ والمركَبُ السَّوءُ».

Hadith 8

Artificial scarcity and divine abundance

Muslim collects from Abū Dharr, from Allah's messenger ﷺ, from that which he relates directly from his Lord that He said in a long hadith:

"O My slaves, if the first and the last of you, the men and the jinn of you were to all gather in one place and were to ask of Me, and I were to give each of them what he asked for, that would not decrease from My dominion more than a needle can decrease from the ocean when dipped in it."

الحديث الثامن

الندرة مصطنعة والفضل إلهي

رَوى مسلم عَنْ أَبِي ذَرٍّ، عَنِ النبي ﷺ، فِيمَا رَوَى عَنِ اللهِ تَبَارَكَ وَتَعَالَى أَنَّهُ قَالَ في حديث طويل:

«يَا عِبَادِي لَوْ أَنَّ أَوَّلَكُمْ وَآخِرَكُمْ وَإِنْسَكُمْ وَجِنَّكُمْ قَامُوا فِي صَعِيدٍ وَاحِدٍ فَسَأَلُونِي فَأَعْطَيْتُ كُلَّ إِنْسَانٍ مَسْأَلَتَهُ، مَا نَقَصَ ذَلِكَ مِمَّا عِنْدِي إِلَّا كَمَا يَنْقُصُ الْمِخْيَطُ إِذَا أُدْخِلَ الْبَحْرَ».

Hadith 9

Seek sustenance though permitted means and leaving off avarice

Abū Nuʿaym collects in his Ḥilya from Abū Umāma: the Prophet ﷺ said:

"Indeed, the Holy Spirit has breathed into me this inspiration: Surely a soul will not die until it completes its appointed time and receives its sustenance. So be mindful of Allah and seek beautifully. Never should the delay of sustenance drive one of you to seek it through disobedience to Allah. Indeed Allah the Most High and what is with Him is not attained except through His obedience."

It was narrated as well by Ibn Majah, al-Hakim, and al-Bayhaqi in al-Kubra from Jabir b. Abdullah. Shaikh Muhammad Nasir al-Din al-Albani said in his grading of "Fiqh al-Sira": It is Sahih, having been narrated from numerous chains that strengthen each other.

الحديث التاسع

طلب الرزق بمباشرة الأسباب المشروعة وترك المبالغة في الحرص

روى أبو نعيم في حليته عن أبي أمامة أن النبي ﷺ قال:

«إنَّ رُوحَ القُدُسِ نفثَ في رُوعِي ، أنَّ نفسًا لَن تموتَ حتَّى تستكملَ أجلَها ، وتستوعِبَ رزقَها ، فاتَّقوا اللهَ ، وأجمِلُوا في الطَّلَبِ ، ولا يَحمِلَنَّ أحدَكم استبطاءُ الرِّزقِ أن يطلُبَه بمَعصيةِ اللهِ ، فإنَّ اللهَ تعالى لا يُنالُ ما عندَه إلَّا بطاعتِه.»

ورواه ابن ماجه والحاكم والبيهقي في الكبرى من حديث جابر بن عبدالله. وقال الشيخ محمد ناصر الدين الألباني في تخريج فقه السيرة : صحيح جاء من طرق يقوي بعضها بعضا.

Hadith 10

Otherworldly reward is contingent on worldly benefit

Al-Bukhari collects from al-Miqdām ibn Maʿdīyakrib al-Zubaydī, from Allah's messenger ﷺ who said:

"No one has ever consumed food better than that which he has earned with his own hands and the Prophet of Allah David – peace be upon him - would eat from the work of his own hands."

It is present in Ibn Mājah with the wording:

"A man has never earned any earnings more wholesome than the work of his own hand and whatever a man spends on himself, his wife, his children, and his servant is an act of charity."

الحديث العاشر

الأجر الأخروي مترتب على النفع الدنيوي

روى البخاري عَنْ المِقْدَامِ بْنِ مَعْدِيكَرِبَ الزُّبَيْدِيِّ عَنْ رَسُولِ اللَّهِ ﷺ قَالَ:

«مَا أَكَلَ أَحَدٌ طَعَامًا قَطُّ، خَيْرًا مِنْ أَنْ يَأْكُلَ مِنْ عَمَلِ يَدِهِ، وَإِنَّ نَبِيَّ اللَّهِ دَاوُدَ عَلَيْهِ السَّلَامِ، كَانَ يَأْكُلُ مِنْ عَمَلِ يَدِهِ.»

وهو عند ابن ماجه بلفظ:

«مَا كَسَبَ الرَّجُلُ كَسْبًا أَطْيَبَ مِنْ عَمَلِ يَدِهِ وَمَا أَنْفَقَ الرَّجُلُ عَلَى نَفْسِهِ وَأَهْلِهِ وَوَلَدِهِ وَخَادِمِهِ فَهُوَ صَدَقَةٌ.»

Hadith 11

The Most High's statement:
Beautified for man is love of desires.

Al-Bukhārī collects from Ḥakim ibn Ḥizām who said: I asked the Prophet, and he gave me, and then again, I asked him, and he gave me, and then again, I asked him, and he gave me and he then said,

"O Ḥakim! This wealth is green and sweet, and whoever takes it with a sense of appreciation, he will be blessed in it. But whoever takes it with entitlement, it will not be blessed, and he will be like the one who eats but is never satisfied. And the upper hand is better than the lower hand."

الحديث الحادي عشر

قوله تعالى : زُيِّنَ لِلنَّاسِ حُبُّ الشَّهَوَاتِ

رَوى البخاري عن حَكِيم بْنَ حِزَامٍ رَضِيَ اللَّهُ عَنْهُ، قَالَ: سَأَلْتُ رَسُولَ اللَّهِ ﷺ، فَأَعْطَانِي، ثُمَّ سَأَلْتُهُ، فَأَعْطَانِي، ثُمَّ سَأَلْتُهُ، فَأَعْطَانِي ثُمَّ قَالَ:

«يَا حَكِيمُ، إِنَّ هَذَا المَالَ خَضِرَةٌ حُلْوَةٌ، فَمَنْ أَخَذَهُ بِسَخَاوَةِ نَفْسٍ بُورِكَ لَهُ فِيهِ، وَمَنْ أَخَذَهُ بِإِشْرَافِ نَفْسٍ لَمْ يُبَارَكْ لَهُ فِيهِ، كَالَّذِي يَأْكُلُ وَلاَ يَشْبَعُ، اليَدُ العُلْيَا خَيْرٌ مِنَ اليَدِ السُّفْلَى.»

Hadith 12

The Most High's statement: Never do you spend anything except that Allah repays it; and He is the best of Sustainers

Muslim collects from Abū Hurayra: from Allah's messenger ﷺ who said:

"Charity does not in any way decrease the wealth and the servant who pardons, Allah only increases his honor, and the one who shows humility, Allah only elevates him in the estimation of the people."

الحديث الثاني عشر

قوله تعالى : وما أنفقتم من شيء فهو يخلفه وهو خير الرازقين ...الآية

رَوى مسلم عَنْ أَبِي هُرَيْرَةَ، عَنْ رَسُولِ اللهِ ﷺ، قَالَ:

«مَا نَقَصَتْ صَدَقَةٌ مِنْ مَالٍ، وَمَا زَادَ اللهُ عَبْدًا بِعَفْوٍ، إِلَّا عِزًّا، وَمَا تَوَاضَعَ أَحَدٌ لِلَّهِ إِلَّا رَفَعَهُ اللهُ.»

Hadith 13

The Most High's Statement: Do not devour your wealth between you through deceit

Al-Bukhārī collects from Abū Hurayra, from the Prophet ﷺ who said:

"Whoever takes people's wealth with the objective to pay it back, Allah will pay it back for him. And whoever takes it with the objective of destroying it, Allah will destroy him."

الحديث الثالث عشر

قوله تعالى: وَلَا تَأْكُلُوا أَمْوَالَكُمْ بَيْنَكُمْ بِالْبَاطِلِ

روى البخاري عن أبي هريرة، رضي الله عنه، عن النبي ﷺ قال:

«مَن أَخَذَ أَمْوالَ النَّاسِ يُرِيدُ أداءَها أدَّى اللَّهُ عنْه، ومَن أَخَذَ إتْلافَها أتْلَفَهُ اللَّهُ.»

Hadith 14

The reasons for unknown outcomes in sales are nonexistence, inability to deliver, or indefinite terms

Muslim collects from Abū Hurayra who said:

Allah's messenger ﷺ forbade the Pebble sale and the Gharar sale.

Al-Azhari – Allah have mercy on him – said: Gharar is anything based on an unreliable undertaking; included in this is all transactions which transactors cannot reckon the reality of due to something unknown. Al-Hamīdi said about the Pebble sale: It

is when throwing pebbles from one of the transactors' hands is a sign the sale is complete.

الحديث الرابع عشر

أسباب ما لا تعلم عاقبته في التبادل هو العدم والعجز عن التسليم والجهل بمقتضيات العقد

روى مسلم عَنْ أبي هُرَيْرَةَ :

قَالَ نَهَى رَسُولُ اللَّهِ ﷺ عَنْ بَيْعِ الْحَصَاةِ وَعَنْ بَيْعِ الْغَرَرِ.

وَقَالَ الْأَزْهَرِيُّ – رَحِمَهُ اللَّهُ –: الْغَرَرُ مَا كَانَ عَلَى غَيْرِ عَهْدٍ وَثِقَةٍ، وَيَدْخُلُ فِيهِ الْبُيُوعُ الَّتِي لَا يُحِيطُ بِكُنْهِهَا الْمُتَبَايِعَانِ مِنْ كُلِّ مَجْهُولٍ. وقال الحميدي في بيع الحصاة : هو أن يكون رمي الْحَصَاة من يَد أحد الْمُتَبَايعين عَلَامَة لتَمَام البيع.

Hadith 15

**The Most High's statement:
O you who believe, fear Allah and leave off whatever
remains of Riba if you are truly believers.**

Muslim collects from Jābir:

Allah's messenger ﷺ cursed the person who pays Ribā, the
one who it is paid to, its scribe, and its two witnesses. He said,
"They are all the same."

الحديث الخامس عشر

قوله تعالى: يَاأَيُّهَا الَّذِينَ آمَنُوا اتَّقُوا اللَّهَ
وَذَرُوا مَا بَقِيَ مِنَ الرِّبَا إِنْ كُنْتُمْ مُؤْمِنِينَ ...الآية

روى مسلم عَنْ جَابِر قَالَ:

لَعَنَ رَسُولُ اللَّهِ ﷺ آكِلَ الرِّبَا وَمُوكِلَهُ وَكَاتِبَهُ وَشَاهِدَيْهِ
وَقَالَ : «هُمْ سَوَاءٌ.»

Hadith 16

Wealth is three types: nonfungible, semi-fungible and fungible

Muslim collects from ʿUbāda ibn al-Ṣāmit who said:

Indeed I heard Allah's messenger ﷺ forbid the sale of gold for gold, silver for silver, wheat for wheat, barley for barley, dates for dates, salt for salt, except in like for like, asset for asset; so whoever increases or seeks increase has committed Ribā.

In another wording: "When these types are different, then sell as you wish if it is hand to hand."

الحديث السادس عشر

الأموال أنواع ثلاثة متفاوتة ومتقاربة ومتساوية

روى مسلم عَنْ عُبَادَةَ بْنِ الصَّامِتِ قال إني سمعت رسول الله ﷺ:

« يَنْهَى عن بَيْعِ الذَّهَبِ بالذَّهَبِ، وَالْفِضَّةِ بالفِضَّةِ، وَالْبُرِّ بالبُرِّ، وَالشَّعِيرِ بالشَّعِيرِ، وَالتَّمْرِ بالتَّمْرِ، وَالمِلْحِ بالمِلْحِ، إِلَّا سَوَاءً بِسَوَاءٍ، عَيْنًا بعَيْنٍ، فمَن زَادَ، أَو ازْدَادَ، فقَدْ أَرْبَى.»

وفي لفظ: «فَإِذَا اخْتَلَفَتْ هَذِهِ الأَصْنَافُ فَبِيعُوا كَيْفَ شِئْتُمْ إِذَا كَانَ يَدًا بِيَدِ.»

Hadith 17

What is permitted in appearance yet leads to something forbidden is forbidden

Al-Tirmidhī collects from ʿAbdullāh ibn Amr, that Allah's messenger ﷺ said:

"A loan with a sale is not permitted, nor two conditions in a sale, nor gain from no liability, nor sale of what is not with you."

Abu Eisa al-Tirmidhi said: This is a Hasan Sahih hadith.

الحديث السابع عشر

ما ظاهره الإباحة من الذرائع فتؤول إلى المحرَّم محرَّم

روى التِّرمذي عن عبد الله بن عمرو ﷺ : أن رسول الله ﷺ قال :

« لا يحِلُّ سلَفٌ وبيعٌ ولا شرطانِ في بيعٍ ولا ربحُ ما لم يُضمَنْ ولا بيعُ ما ليسَ عندَكَ. »

وقال أبو عيسى التِّرمذي : حديث حسن صحيح.

Hadith 18

All Muslims hold consensus that selling debt for debt is impermissible

Al-Bayhaqī collects from Ibn ʿUmar:

The Prophet 🕊 forbade selling arrears for arrears.

This hadith is weak, its defect being Musa b. Ubaida. From Imam Ahmad who said: There is no sound hadith on this, yet the consensus of the people is that it is impermissible to sell debt for debt.

In the Muwaṭṭaʾ of Malik: Arrears for arrears is when a man sells a debt that he owes someone else for a debt that is owed to another person.

الحديث الثامن عشر

أَجْمَعَ الْمُسْلِمُونَ عَلَى مَنْعِ بيع الدَّيْنِ بِالدَّيْن

روى البيهقي عَن ابْن عُمَرَ :

أَنَّ النَّبِيَّ ﷺ نَهَى عَنْ بَيْعِ الْكَالِئِ بِالْكَالِئِ.

وهذا الحديث ضعيف ، وعلته موسى بن عبيدة ، وعن الإمام أحمد قال : ليس في هذا حديث يصح لكن إجماع الناس على أنه لا يجوز بيع دين بدين.

وفي موطأ الإمام مالك: والكالئ بالكالئ أن يبيع الرجل دينا له على رجل بدين على رجل آخر.

Hadith 19

Deferred countervalues in sales are not included in selling debt for debt

Al-Bukhari and Muslim collected from Jabir b. 'Abdullah who related that:

He was "...riding on his camel which had grown feeble and he wanted to set it free. The Prophet ﷺ caught up to me, supplicated for me, and smacked the camel. It took off like I had never seen before. He ﷺ then said, "Sell it to me for one Uqiya." I replied, " No." He ﷺ again said, "Sell it to me." So I sold it to him for an Uqiya on the condition I ride it home to my family. When I reached al-Madina, I took the camel to him, and he paid me for it. I returned to my family, and he sent someone to fetch me. When I came, he said, "Did you think that I haggled with you in order to take your camel? Take your camel and the dirhams, they belong to you." This is Muslim's wording.

I say: An Uqiya is forty dirhams. On this topic in the two sahihs is the hadith from Ibn Umar about the Istisna' of a ring, and the hadith of Sahl about the building of his Minbar ﷺ, and connected to this is what was related from Ibn Abbas about the Salam sale.

الحديث التاسع عشر

تَأْجيل البَدَلين في البُيوع لَيس مِن بَيع الدَّيْنُ بِالدَّيْن

روى الشيخان عَنْ جَابِرِ بْنِ عَبْدِالله

أنَّهُ كَانَ عَلَى جَمَل لَهُ قَدْ أَعْيَى. فَأَرَادَ أَنْ يُسيِّبَهُ. قَالَ: فَلَحِقَني النَّبيُّ ﷺ، فَدَعَا لي، وَضَرَبَهُ. فَسَارَ سَيْراً لَمْ يَسِرْ مِثْلَهُ، فَقَالَ : "بعْنيه بأُوقيَّةٍ" قُلْتُ : لا. ثمَّ قَالَ : "بِعْنيه" فَبِعْتُهُ بأُوقيَّةٍ، واشْتَرَطْتُ حُمْلانَهُ إلى أَهْلي، فَلَمَّا بَلَغْتُ أَتَيْتُهُ بالجَمَل، فَنَقَدَني ثَمَنَهُ، ثمَّ رَجَعْتُ فَأَرْسَلَ في أَثَري. فَقَالَ : "أَتُراني مَاكَسْتُكَ لآخُذَ جَمَلَكَ؟ خُذْ جَمَلَكَ وَدَراهِمَكَ. فَهُوَ لَكَ." و هذا السّياق لمسلم.

قلت: الأوقية أربعون درهما ، وفي الباب عندهما عن ابن عمر في استصناع خاتم، ومن حديث سهل في صنع منبره ﷺ، ويلحق بذلك ما ورد عن ابن عباس في بيع السلم.

Hadith 20

Inefficiencies can ensure fair pricing and prevent exploitation

Al-Bukhārī collects from Abū Saʿīd al-Khudrī and Abū Hurayra:

Allah's messenger ﷺ assigned a man over Khaibar, who then came to him with high quality dates. Allah's messenger ﷺ said "Are all the dates of Khaibar like this?

He replied "No, by Allah O Allah's messenger ﷺ. We get a Ṣāʿ of these for two Ṣāʿ, and two Ṣāʿ for three."

Allah's messenger ﷺ then said "Do not do this. Sell the mix for dirhams, then with the dirhams purchase high quality dates."

In another narration from Abū Saʿīd in Al-Bukhārī "Oof, oof, the epitome of Ribā. Don't do this...."

I say: A Ṣāʿ is unit of measure equal to four mudd equal to 2.06 liters according to the majority.

الحديث العشرون

عدم الكفاءة قد يضمن التسعير العادل ويمنع الاستغلال

روى البخاري عن أبي سَعِيدٍ الْخُدْرِيِّ وَعَنْ أَبِي هُرَيْرَةَ رَضِيَ اللهُ عَنْهُما :

أَنَّ رَسُولَ اللهِ ﷺ اسْتَعْمَلَ رَجُلًا عَلَى خَيْبَرَ فَجَاءَهُ بِتَمْرٍ جَنِيبٍ فَقَالَ رَسُولُ اللهِ ﷺ «أَكُلُّ تَمْرِ خَيْبَرَ هَكَذَا؟» قَالَ لَا وَاللهِ يَا رَسُولَ اللهِ إِنَّا لَنَأْخُذُ الصَّاعَ مِنْ هَذَا بِالصَّاعَيْنِ وَالصَّاعَيْنِ بِالثَّلَاثَةِ. فَقَالَ رَسُولُ اللهِ ﷺ : «لَا تَفْعَلْ بِعِ الْجَمْعَ بِالدَّرَاهِمِ ثُمَّ ابْتَعْ بِالدَّرَاهِمِ جَنِيبًا».

وفي رواية لأبي سعيد في البخاري «أَوَّهْ أَوَّهْ عَيْنُ الرِّبَا لَا تَفْعَلْ.»

قلت: الصاع وحدة قياس تساوي أربعة أمداد تساوي 2.06 لتر على قول الجمهور.

Hadith 21

The Riba of Pre-Islamic Ignorance is their statement: You either pay or you increase

Al-Ḥārith collects in his *Musnad* from ʿUmāra Al-Hamdāni who said I heard ʿAlī say: Allah's messenger ﷺ said,

"Every loan that accrues a benefit it is Ribā."

It was narrated in Marfūʿ form by al-Ḥārith in his Musnad. Ibn Ḥajar said: It's isnād is despicable, and it has a weak corroborating narration. It was narrated by al-Bayhaqī in Mawqūf form from Ibn Masʿūd, Ibn ʿAbbās, and others.

الحديث الحادي والعشرون

ربا الجاهلية قولهم إما أن تقضي وإما أن تربي

روى الحارث في مسنده عَنْ عُمَارَةَ الْهَمْدَانِيِّ قَالَ: سَمِعْتُ عَلِيًّا يَقُولُ: قَالَ رَسُولُ اللَّهِ ﷺ:

«كُلُّ قَرْضٍ جَرَّ مَنْفَعَةً فَهُوَ رِبًا.»

هكذا مرفوعا عند الحارث في مسنده وقال الحافظ ابن حجر: إسناده ساقط، وله شاهد ضعيف. وقد رواه البيهقي موقوفا على ابن مَسْعُود وابْنِ عَبَّاس وغيرهما.

Hadith 22

Forbidden artifice is that which undermines a Sharia principle and negates a legislated benefit

Aḥmad collects in his Musnad from Ibn ʿAbbās:

The Prophet ﷺ was sitting in the masjid facing his home. He then looked to the sky and laughed, then said:

"Allah cursed the Jews; fat was forbidden for them but instead they sold it and ate the price. Indeed when Allah mighty and high forbids a people from consuming something he forbids its price for them as well."

الحديث الثاني والعشرون

الحيلة المحرمة ما هدم أصلاً شرعياً وناقض مصلحة شرعية

روى أحمد في مسنده عن ابنُ عَبَّاس، قَالَ:

كَانَ رَسُولُ اللهِ ﷺ، قَاعِدًا فِي المَسْجِدِ مُسْتَقْبِلًا الحُجَرَ، قَالَ: فَنَظَرَ إِلَى السَّمَاءِ، فَضَحِكَ، ثُمَّ قَالَ:

«لَعَنَ اللهُ الْيَهُودَ، حُرِّمَتْ عَلَيْهِمُ الشُّحُومُ فَبَاعُوهَا، وَأَكَلُوا أَثْمَانَهَا، وَإِنَّ اللهَ عَزَّ وَجَلَّ إِذَا حَرَّمَ عَلَى قَوْمٍ أَكْلَ شَيْءٍ حَرَّمَ عَلَيْهِمْ ثَمَنَهُ.»

Hadith 23

**Any flesh sustained by the illicit,
then the Hellfire has more right to it.**

Ibn Ḥibbān collects from Abū Hurayra who said, Allah's messenger ﷺ said

"Whoever accumulates Ḥarām wealth, then gives it in charity, he will have no reward for it, and its sin will be on him."

الحديث الثالث والعشرون

أي لحم نبت من سحت فالنار أولى به

روى ابن حبان عَنْ أَبِي هُرَيْرَةَ، قَالَ: قَالَ رَسُولُ اللَّهِ ﷺ:

«مَنْ جَمَعَ مَالًا حَرَامًا، ثُمَّ تَصَدَّقَ بِهِ، لَمْ يَكُنْ لَهُ فِيهِ أجر، وكان إصره عليه.»

Hadith 24

Prohibitions related to the rights of man are based on protecting those rights and preventing harm

Muslim collects from Abū Hurayra said: Allah's messenger ﷺ said:

"Do not envy one another. Do not raise prices on one another. Do not despise one another. Do not turn away from one another. None should preempt his brother's sale; Be slaves of Allah, brothers. The Muslim is the brother of a Muslim: he does not oppress him, he does not demean him, he does not humiliate him. Taqwā is right here – pointing to his chest thrice - it is enough evil for a man to demean his Muslim brother. The entirety of a Muslim is forbidden for another Muslim: his blood, his wealth, and his honor."

الحديث الرابع والعشرون

المحظورات العائدة إلى حقوق العباد مبناها صيانة الحق ومنع الإيذاء

روى مسلم عَنْ أَبِى هُرَيْرَةَ قَالَ قَالَ رَسُولُ اللَّهِ ﷺ :

«لاَ تَحَاسَدُوا وَلاَ تَنَاجَشُوا وَلاَ تَبَاغَضُوا وَلاَ تَدَابَرُوا وَلاَ يَبِعْ بَعْضُكُمْ عَلَى بَيْعِ بَعْضٍ وَكُونُوا عِبَادَ اللَّهِ إِخْوَانًا. الْمُسْلِمُ أَخُو الْمُسْلِمِ لاَ يَظْلِمُهُ وَلاَ يَخْذُلُهُ وَلاَ يَحْقِرُهُ. التَّقْوَى هَا هُنَا - وَيُشِيرُ إِلَى صَدْرِهِ ثَلاَثَ مَرَّاتٍ - بِحَسْبِ امْرِئٍ مِنَ الشَّرِّ أَنْ يَحْقِرَ أَخَاهُ الْمُسْلِمَ كُلُّ الْمُسْلِمِ عَلَى الْمُسْلِمِ حَرَامٌ دَمُهُ وَمَالُهُ وَعِرْضُهُ».

Hadith 25

The Most High's statement: Have you seen the one that takes his desires as his god?

Al-Bukhārī collects from Abū Hurayra: Allah's messenger ﷺ said:

"Destroyed is the slave of the Dīnār, the Dirham, the shirt, and the jacket; if he is given, he's pleased and if not then he is not pleased."

الحديث الخامس والعشرون

قوله تعالى: أَفَرَأَيْتَ مَنِ اتَّخَذَ إِلَهَهُ هَوَاهُ

روى البخاري عَنْ أَبِي هُرَيْرَةَ رَضِيَ اللَّهُ عَنْهُ، قَالَ: قَالَ رَسُولُ اللَّهِ ﷺ:

«تَعِسَ عَبْدُ الدِّينَارِ، وَالدِّرْهَمِ، وَالْقَطِيفَةِ، وَالْخَمِيصَةِ، إِنْ أُعْطِيَ رَضِيَ، وَإِنْ لَمْ يُعْطَ لَمْ يَرْضَ».

Hadith 26

A change of hands necessitates a change in ruling

Al-Bukhārī collects from Anas ibn Mālik who said:

The Prophet ﷺ was brought some meat. It was said "It was given as Ṣadaqa to Barīra." He replied, "It was Ṣadaqa for her and for us a gift."

الحديث السادس والعشرون

اختلاف اليد يستلزم اختلاف الحكم

روى البخاري عَنْ أَنَس بْن مَالِكٍ رَضِىَ اللَّهُ عَنْهُ ، قَالَ :

أُتِيَ النبي ﷺ بلَحْمٍ فَقِيلَ تُصُدِّقَ عَلَى بَرِيرَةَ ، قَالَ « هُوَ لَهَا صَدَقَةٌ وَلَنَا هَدِيَّةٌ.»

Hadith 27

Prohibition of deception
and showing things in ways they are not

Al-Tirmidhī collects from Abū Hurayra:

The Prophet ﷺ passed a mound of wheat and stuck his hand in it. When he found his fingers wet, he asked "Merchant of this wheat, what's this?" The man replied that "...rain had hit it, O Allah's messenger ﷺ." He said: "Should you not then place it at the top where the people can see it? Whoever cheats is not from us."

The basis of this hadith is found in Muslim.

الحديث السابع والعشرون

تحريم الخداع وإظهار الشيء على غير ما هو عليه

روى التِّرمذي عن أبي هريرة :

أن رسول الله ﷺ مر على صبرة من طعام فأدخل يده فيها فنالت أصابعه بللا فقال « يا صاحب الطعام ! ما هذا ؟» قال أصابته السماء يا رسول الله ! قال « أفلا جعلته فوق الطعام حتى يراه الناس ؟» ثم قال « من غَشَّ فَلَيْسَ مِنَّا.»

وأصل الحديث في صحيح مسلم.

Hadith 28

Values are at the heart of business

Al-Bukhārī collects from Ḥakīm ibn Ḥizām said: Allah's messenger ﷺ said:

"Transactors have the option as long as they don't separate. If they are truthful and transparent their transaction will be blessed. If they hide and lie, the blessing of their transaction will be wiped out."

الحديث الثامن والعشرون

القيم هي في صميم الأعمال

روى البخاري عَنْ حَكِيمِ بْنِ حِزَامٍ، رَضِيَ اللَّهُ عَنْهُ، قَالَ: قَالَ رَسُولُ اللهِ ﷺ

«الْبَيِّعَانِ بِالْخِيَارِ مَا لَمْ يَتَفَرَّقَا فَإِنْ صَدَقَا وَبَيَّنَا بُورِكَ لَهُمَا فِي بَيْعِهِمَا وَإِنْ كَتَمَا وَكَذَبَا مُحِقَتْ بَرَكَةُ بَيْعِهِمَا.»

Hadith 29

Returns follow assets, and liability is based on ownership and rights

Al-Tirmidhī collects from ʿĀʾisha:

Allah's messenger ﷺ decreed that returns are contingent on liability.

Abu Isa al-Tirmidhi said: This is a Hasan Sahih hadith. The explanation of "returns are contingent on liability" is a man who purchases a slave then puts him to work, then finds a defect in him, so he returns him to the seller. The gains made here are for the purchaser, as the slave if it had died, would have died while property of the purchaser. Issues similar to his are meant by "returns are contingent on liability."

الحديث التاسع والعشرون

الخراج تابع للأصل والضمان تابع للملك والاستحقاق

روى التِّرمذي عَنْ عَائِشَةَ قَالَتْ:

قَضَى رَسُولُ اللهِ ﷺ: « أَنَّ الخَرَاجَ بِالضَّمَانِ.»

قال أبو عيسى التِّرمذي: هذا حديث حسن صحيح. وتفسير الخراج بالضمان هو الرجل الذي يشتري العبد ويستغله ثم يجد به عيبا فيرده على البائع فالغلة للمشتري لأن العبد لو هلك من مال المشتري ونحو هذا من المسائل يكون فيه الخراج بالضمان.

Hadith 30

The principle of removing harm
and Free market economics

al-Tirmidhi collects from Anas:

Prices became excessive during the time of Allah's messenger ﷺ, so they said: "O Allah's messenger ﷺ! Set prices for us!" So he said:

"Indeed Allah is Al-Musaʿir, Al-Qābiḍ, Al-Bāsiṭ, Ar-Razzāq. And I am hopeful that I meet my Lord and none of you are seek me out for an injustice involving blood or wealth."

Abu Isa al-Tirmidhi said: This is a Hasan Sahih hadith.

الحديث الثلاثون

قاعدة الضرر يزال واقتصاديات السوق الحرة

روى الترمذي عَنْ أَنَسٍ قَالَ:

غَلَا السِّعْرُ عَلَى عَهْدِ رَسُولِ اللهِ ﷺ، فَقَالُوا: يَا رَسُولَ اللهِ، سَعِّرْ لَنَا، فَقَالَ:

«إِنَّ اللَّهَ هُوَ المُسَعِّرُ، القَابِضُ، البَاسِطُ، الرَّزَّاقُ، وَإِنِّي لَأَرْجُو أَنْ أَلْقَى رَبِّي وَلَيْسَ أَحَدٌ مِنْكُمْ يَطْلُبُني بِمَظْلِمَةٍ فِي دَمٍ وَلَا مَالٍ.»

قال أبو عيسى هذا حديث حسن صحيح.

Hadith 31

Time is a scarce resource

Al-Bukhārī collects in his Al-Adab al-Mufrad from Anas: from the Prophet ﷺ who said:

"If the Hour is nigh and you have a seedling in your hand, then if you are able to plant it before your stand up, then plant it."

الحديث الحادي والثلاثون

الزمن مورد نادر

روى البخاري في الأدب المفرد عن أنس عن النبي ﷺ قال:

«إنْ قامَتِ الساعةُ وفي يدِ أحدِكمْ فَسِيلةٌ، فإنِ استطاعَ أنْ لا تقومَ حتى يَغرِسَها فلْيغرِسْهَا».

Hadith 32

Preservation of Capital is an Objective of the Sharia

Ahmad collects in his Musnad from Sa'id b. Hurayth who said: I heard Allah's messenger ﷺ say:

"Whoever sells property deserves not to be blessed therein unless he places it into something similar or akin to it."

Shaikh Shu'ayb al-Arna'ut said: It is a Hasan hadith due to its supporting and corroborating narrations.

Al-Sindi said: The meaning of this hadith is that the value will vanish, leaving the person with no home and no money.

الحديث الثاني والثلاثون

حفظ المال مقصد شرعي

روى أحمد في مسنده عن سعيد بن حريث قال: سمعت قال رسول الله ﷺ:

«مَنْ بَاعَ عَقَارًا كَانَ قَمِنًا أَنْ لَا يُبَارَكَ لَهُ، إِلَّا أَنْ يَجْعَلَهُ فِي مِثْلِهِ أَوْ غَيْرِهِ.»

قال الشيخ شعيب الأرنؤوط: حديث حسن بمبابعاته وشواهده.

قال السندي: ومعنى الحديث: أن الغالب أن الثمن ينصرف، فيبقى الإنسان بلا دار وبلا ثمن.

Hadith 33

Civil dealings and customs remain permitted as long as they do not contravene a Shariah principle

Muslim collects from Anas: the Prophet ﷺ passed by a people pollinating and said,

"If you didn't, it would work."[6] It resulted in a bad harvest. He passed by them and said: "What is with your trees?" They replied: You said such and such. He said: "You know better the affairs of your world."

---

[6] - The Arabic here can be understood in two ways, given the context and understanding of the listener, as either a question "would it work?" or as a statement "it would work." I've chosen the latter given the reaction of the farmers mentioned in the Hadith.

الحديث الثالث والثلاثون

المعاملات والعادات باقيةٌ على الأصل ما لم تخالف أصلاً شرعياً

روى مسلم عَنْ أَنَسٍ أَنَّ النَّبيَّ ﷺ مَرَّ بِقَوْمٍ يُلَقِّحُونَ فَقَالَ :

« لَوْ لَمْ تَفْعَلُوا لَصَلُحَ.» قَالَ فَخَرَجَ شِيصًا فَمَرَّ بِهِمْ فَقَالَ « مَا لِنَخْلِكُمْ؟» قَالُوا قُلْتَ كَذَا وَكَذَا قَالَ «أَنْتُمْ أَعْلَمُ بِأَمْرِ دُنْيَاكُمْ.»

Hadith 34

The basis of partnerships is the sharing of risk and reward

Abu Dawud from Abu Hurayah in Marfū' form:

"Allah says, 'I am the third of two partners as long as one of them does not cheat the other; when he cheats him I leave from among them.'"

Abu Dawud was silent about this hadith, and al-Hakim said "This hadith has a Sahih chain, and it was not collected by them both" - meaning Bukhari and Muslim – and al-Dhahabi agreed.

الحديث الرابع والثلاثون

الأصل في الشركة الاشتراك في المغنم والمغرم

روى أبو داود عَنْ أَبِى هُرَيْرَةَ رَفَعَهُ قَالَ:

« إِنَّ اللَّهَ يَقُولُ أَنَا ثَالِثُ الشَّرِيكَيْنِ مَا لَمْ يَخُنْ أَحَدُهُمَا صَاحِبَهُ فَإِذَا خَانَهُ خَرَجْتُ مِنْ بَيْنِهِمَا ».

وسكت عنه أبو داود، وقال الحاكم هذا حديث صحيح الإسناد و لم يخرجاه، – أي البخاري ومسلم – ووافقه الذهبي.

Hadith 35

Budgeting and Saving is from the Sunna

Al-Bukhārī collects from Abū Hurayra, from the Prophet ﷺ who said:

"If I had Mount Uḥud in gold, I'd not want three to pass except that not a single dīnār of it was left with me if I can find someone who will accept it from me, not including something I've saved to pay a debt I owe."

الحديث الخامس والثلاثون

موازنة الدخل والتوفير من السنة النبوية

روى البخاري عن أبي هُرَيْرَةَ، عَنِ النبي ﷺ قَالَ:

«لَوْ كَانَ عِنْدِي أُحُدٌ ذَهَبًا لأَحْبَبْتُ أَنْ لاَ يَأْتِيَ ثَلاَثٌ وَعِنْدِي مِنْهُ دِينَارٌ لَيْسَ شَيْءٌ أَرْصُدُهُ فِي دَيْنٍ عَلَيَّ أَجِدُ مَنْ يَقْبَلُهُ.»

Hadith 36

Every action that brings about harm or prevents some good, then it is forbidden

Al-Bukhārī collects from Abū Hurayra who said:

By Allah, the One Whom there is none worthy of worship besides Him – I would lay on the ground on my side due to hunger, and I would fasten a stone to my stomach out of hunger. One day I sat by the path they would pass by. Abū Bakr passed and so I asked him about a verse from Allah's Book, not asking except that he might feed me. But he passed on without doing so. Then 'Umar passed, so I asked him about a verse from Allah's Book, not asking except that he might feed me. But he passed on without doing so.

Then Abū-l-Qāsim ﷺ passed by. He smiled when he saw me – seeing the need in me and in my face - and said: "O Abū Hirr!" I said: "At your service O Allah's messenger ﷺ!" He said: "Come along." He continued and I followed him. He entered his home, so I sought permission to enter, and he permitted me. He found a bowl of milk and said: "Where did this milk come from?" It was said: "It was a gift to you from so – and – so."

الحديث السادس والثلاثون

كل تصرف جر فسادا أو دفع صلاحا فهو منهي عنه

رَوَى البُخَارِيُّ أَنَّ أَبَا هُرَيْرَةَ، كَانَ يَقُولُ:

آللَّهِ الَّذِي لاَ إِلَهَ إِلَّا هُوَ، إِنْ كُنْتُ لَأَعْتَمِدُ بِكَبِدِي عَلَى الأَرْضِ مِنَ الجُوعِ، وَإِنْ كُنْتُ لَأَشُدُّ الحَجَرَ عَلَى بَطْنِي مِنَ الجُوعِ، وَلَقَدْ قَعَدْتُ يَوْمًا عَلَى طَرِيقِهِمُ الَّذِي يَخْرُجُونَ مِنْهُ، فَمَرَّ أَبُو بَكْرٍ، فَسَأَلْتُهُ عَنْ آيَةٍ مِنْ كِتَابِ اللَّهِ، مَا سَأَلْتُهُ إِلَّا لِيُشْبِعَنِي، فَمَرَّ وَلَمْ يَفْعَلْ، ثُمَّ مَرَّ بِي عُمَرُ، فَسَأَلْتُهُ عَنْ آيَةٍ مِنْ كِتَابِ اللَّهِ، مَا سَأَلْتُهُ إِلَّا لِيُشْبِعَنِي، فَمَرَّ فَلَمْ يَفْعَلْ.

ثُمَّ مَرَّ بِي أَبُو القَاسِمِ ﷺ، فَتَبَسَّمَ حِينَ رَآنِي، وَعَرَفَ مَا فِي نَفْسِي وَمَا فِي وَجْهِي، ثُمَّ قَالَ: «يَا أَبَا هِرٍّ» قُلْتُ: لَبَّيْكَ يَا رَسُولَ اللَّهِ، قَالَ: «الحَقْ» وَمَضَى فَتَبِعْتُهُ، فَدَخَلَ، فَاسْتَأْذَنَ، فَأَذِنَ لِي، فَدَخَلَ، فَوَجَدَ لَبَنًا فِي قَدَحٍ، فَقَالَ: «مِنْ أَيْنَ هَذَا اللَّبَنُ؟» قَالُوا: أَهْدَاهُ لَكَ فُلَانٌ أَوْ فُلَانَةُ.

So Allah's messenger ﷺ said: "O Abū Hirr" I said: "At your service O Allah's messenger ﷺ!" He said: "Go invite the people of As-Ṣuffa for me." He [Abu Hurayra] said: The people of As-Ṣuffa were the guests of Islam; they had no family, wealth, or anyone to rely on. Whenever some charity was brought to him, he would send it to them without taking any of it.

And when a gift was given to him, he would take from it then send for them to share it with them. I became upset and said to myself: What good will this milk do among the people of As-Ṣuffa?! I have more right to drink from this milk at least enough to gain some strength!

So when he came and commanded me, I would serve them, but how much of this milk would actually reach me?! Yet, there was no choice but to obey Allah and obey His Messenger ﷺ, so I went and invited them, and they came. They sought permission to enter, so he allowed them, and they entered and took their seats in the house.

He said: "Abū Hirr!" I responded, "At your service O Allah's messenger ﷺ!" He said, "Take it and serve them." So I took the bowl and gave it to a man who drank his fill then gave it back, then to another who drank his fill then gave it back, until I ended up with Allah's messenger ﷺ, and all of the people had drunk their fill. Allah's messenger ﷺ took the bowl, put it in his hand, then looked to me and smiled.

قَالَ: «أَبَا هِرٍّ» قُلْتُ: لَبَّيْكَ يَا رَسُولَ اللهِ، قَالَ: «الْحَقْ إِلَى أَهْلِ الصُّفَّةِ فَادْعُهُمْ لِي»
قَالَ: وَأَهْلُ الصُّفَّةِ أَضْيَافُ الإِسْلَامِ، لَا يَأْوُونَ إِلَى أَهْلٍ وَلَا مَالٍ وَلَا عَلَى أَحَدٍ،
إِذَا أَتَتْهُ صَدَقَةٌ بَعَثَ بِهَا إِلَيْهِمْ وَلَمْ يَتَنَاوَلْ مِنْهَا شَيْئًا،

وَإِذَا أَتَتْهُ هَدِيَّةٌ أَرْسَلَ إِلَيْهِمْ وَأَصَابَ مِنْهَا وَأَشْرَكَهُمْ فِيهَا، فَسَاءَنِي ذَلِكَ، فَقُلْتُ:
وَمَا هَذَا اللَّبَنُ فِي أَهْلِ الصُّفَّةِ، كُنْتُ أَحَقَّ أَنَا أَنْ أُصِيبَ مِنْ هَذَا اللَّبَنِ شَرْبَةً
أَتَقَوَّى بِهَا.

فَإِذَا جَاءَ أَمَرَنِي، فَكُنْتُ أَنَا أُعْطِيهِمْ، وَمَا عَسَى أَنْ يَبْلُغَنِي مِنْ هَذَا اللَّبَنِ، وَلَمْ يَكُنْ
مِنْ طَاعَةِ اللهِ وَطَاعَةِ رَسُولِهِ ﷺ بُدٌّ، فَأَتَيْتُهُمْ فَدَعَوْتُهُمْ فَأَقْبَلُوا، فَاسْتَأْذَنُوا فَأَذِنَ
هُمْ، وَأَخَذُوا مَجَالِسَهُمْ مِنَ الْبَيْتِ.

قَالَ: «يَا أَبَا هِرٍّ» قُلْتُ: لَبَّيْكَ يَا رَسُولَ اللهِ، قَالَ: «خُذْ فَأَعْطِهِمْ» قَالَ: فَأَخَذْتُ
الْقَدَحَ، فَجَعَلْتُ أُعْطِيهِ الرَّجُلَ فَيَشْرَبُ حَتَّى يَرْوَى، ثُمَّ يَرُدُّ عَلَيَّ الْقَدَحَ، فَأُعْطِيهِ
الرَّجُلَ فَيَشْرَبُ حَتَّى يَرْوَى، ثُمَّ يَرُدُّ عَلَيَّ الْقَدَحَ فَيَشْرَبُ حَتَّى يَرْوَى، ثُمَّ يَرُدُّ عَلَيَّ
الْقَدَحَ، حَتَّى انْتَهَيْتُ إِلَى النَّبِيِّ ﷺ وَقَدْ رَوِيَ الْقَوْمُ كُلُّهُمْ، فَأَخَذَ الْقَدَحَ فَوَضَعَهُ
عَلَى يَدِهِ، فَنَظَرَ إِلَيَّ فَتَبَسَّمَ.

He said: "Abū Hirr!" I responded, "At your service O Allah's messenger ﷺ!" He said, "No one is left but you and I." I replied, "True, O Allah's messenger ﷺ." He said to me, "Sit and drink." So I sat and drank. He then said, "drink." So I drank. He continued to say to me "drink" until I said, "By the One Who sent you with the truth, I have no more space for it!" So I gave him the bowl. He praised Allah, mentioned His name, and drank the remnants.'"

فَقَالَ: «أَبَا هِرٍّ» قُلْتُ: لَبَّيْكَ يَا رَسُولَ اللَّهِ، قَالَ: «بَقِيتُ أَنَا وَأَنْتَ» قُلْتُ: صَدَقْتَ

يَا رَسُولَ اللَّهِ، قَالَ: «اقْعُدْ فَاشْرَبْ» فَقَعَدْتُ فَشَرِبْتُ، فَقَالَ: «اشْرَبْ» فَشَرِبْتُ،

فَمَا زَالَ يَقُولُ: «اشْرَبْ» حَتَّى قُلْتُ: لاَ وَالَّذِي بَعَثَكَ بِالْحَقِّ، مَا أَجِدُ لَهُ مَسْلَكًا،

قَالَ: «فَأَرِنِي» فَأَعْطَيْتُهُ القَدَحَ، فَحَمِدَ اللَّهَ وَسَمَّى وَشَرِبَ الفَضْلَةَ.

Hadith 37

The Most High's statement: O you who believe, when you agree to pay a debt at a future time, then record it

Al-Bukhārī collects from Aisha who said:

Allah's messenger ﷺ died when his shield was pawned to a Jew as collateral for thirty Ṣāʿ of barley for his family.

الحديث السابع والثلاثون

قوله تعالى:

يَا أَيُّهَا الَّذِينَ آمَنُوا إِذَا تَدَايَنتُم بِدَيْنٍ إِلَى أَجَلٍ مُسَمًّى فَاكْتُبُوهُ ...الآية

روى البخاري عَن عائشة، قَالت:

تُوُفِّيَ رَسُولُ اللَّهِ صلى الله عليه وسلم وَدِرْعُهُ مَرْهُونَةٌ عِنْدَ يَهُودِيٍّ بِثَلاَثِينَ صَاعًا مِنْ شَعِيرٍ لأَهْلِهِ .

Hadith 38

The Most High's statement:
If he is in hardship, then respite until solvency

Muslim collects from Ḥudhayfa, that the Prophet ﷺ said:

"A servant from amongst the servants of Allah whom Allah had endowed with riches was brought to Him. He said to him: 'What did you do in the world?' – he said: they cannot conceal anything from Allah - He replied: 'O my Lord, You endowed me with Your wealth. I used to transact with people and it was in my nature to absolve. I showed leniency to the solvent and gave respite to the insolvent,' whereupon Allah said: I have more right to this than you. Absolve my servant."

الحديث الثامن والثلاثون

قوله تعالى: وَإِن كَانَ ذُو عُسْرَةٍ فَنَظِرَةٌ إِلَى مَيْسَرَةٍ

روى مسلم عَنْ حُذَيْفَةَ، أن النبي ﷺ قَالَ:

«أُتِيَ اللهُ بِعَبْدٍ مِنْ عِبَادِهِ آتَاهُ اللهُ مَالًا، فَقَالَ لَهُ: مَاذَا عَمِلْتَ فِي الدُّنْيَا؟ قَالَ: وَلَا يَكْتُمُونَ اللهَ حَدِيثًا، قَالَ: يَا رَبِّ آتَيْتَنِي مَالَكَ، فَكُنْتُ أُبَايِعُ النَّاسَ، وَكَانَ مِنْ خُلُقِي الجَوَازُ، فَكُنْتُ أَتَيَسَّرُ عَلَى المُوسِرِ، وَأُنْظِرُ المُعْسِرَ، فَقَالَ اللهُ: أَنَا أَحَقُّ بِذَا مِنْكَ، تَجَاوَزُوا عَنْ عَبْدِي.»

Hadith 39

Utilizing all means in repaying one's debts

Abū Dāwūd collects from Abū Saʿīd al-Khudrī who said:

One day Allah's messenger 爨 entered the mosque. He saw there a man from the Anṣār called Abū Umāmah. He said: What is the matter that I am seeing you sitting in the mosque when there is no time of prayer? He said: Worries and debts that have ensnared, O Allah's messenger 爨 . He replied: Shall I not teach you words by which, when you say them, Allah will remove your worry and settle your debt? He said: Of course, O Allah's messenger 爨! He said: say in the morning and evening: "O Allah, I seek refuge in You from worry and grief, I seek refuge in You from incapacity and slackness, I seek refuge in You from cowardice and miserliness, and I seek in You from being overcome by debt and being subjugated by man."

He said: When I did that Allah removed my worry and settled my debt.

I say: Abu Dawud was silent about this hadith, and the supplication is narrated in Sahih al-Bukhari from Anas.

الحديث التاسع والثلاثون

أخذ الأسباب لقضاء الديون

روى أبو داود عَنْ أَبِي سَعِيدٍ الْخُدْرِيِّ، قَالَ:

دَخَلَ رَسُولُ صَلَّى عَلَيْهِ وَسَلَّمَ ذَاتَ يَوْمٍ الْمَسْجِدَ، فَإِذَا هُوَ بِرَجُلٍ مِنَ الْأَنْصَارِ، يُقَالُ لَهُ: أَبُو أُمَامَةَ، فَقَالَ: «يَا أُمَامَةَ، مَا لِي أَرَاكَ جَالِسًا فِي الْمَسْجِدِ فِي غَيْرِ وَقْتِ الصَّلَاةِ؟»، قَالَ: هُمُومٌ لَزِمَتْنِي، وَدُيُونٌ يَا رَسُولَ اللَّهِ، قَالَ: «أَفَلَا أُعَلِّمُكَ كَلَامًا إِذَا أَنْتَ قُلْتَهُ أَذْهَبَ اللَّهُ عَزَّ وَجَلَّ هَمَّكَ، وَقَضَى عَنْكَ دَيْنَكَ؟»، قَالَ: قُلْتُ: بَلَى، يَا رَسُولَ، قَالَ: «قُلْ إِذَا أَصْبَحْتَ، وَإِذَا أَمْسَيْتَ: اللَّهُمَّ إِنِّي أَعُوذُ بِكَ مِنَ الْهَمِّ وَالْحَزَنِ، وَأَعُوذُ بِكَ مِنَ الْعَجْزِ وَالْكَسَلِ، وَأَعُوذُ بِكَ مِنَ الْجُبْنِ وَالْبُخْلِ، وَأَعُوذُ بِكَ مِنْ غَلَبَةِ الدَّيْنِ، وَقَهْرِ الرِّجَالِ.»

قَالَ: فَفَعَلْتُ ذَلِكَ، فَأَذْهَبَ اللَّهُ عَزَّ وَجَلَّ هَمِّي، وَقَضَى عَنِّي دَيْنِي.

قلت: سكت عنه أبو داود، والدعاء مروي في صحيح البخاري عن أنس.

Hadith 40

There is consensus that if anyone leaves inheritors, his bequest shall not surpass one third unless they approve

Al-Bukhārī and Muslim collect from Saʿd ibn Abī Waqqāṣ:

Allah's messenger ﷺ visited me during the farewell pilgrimage due to a pain that took me to the edge of death.

I said, "O Allah's Messenger, I am very ill as you see; I am a wealthy man and have no heir except my only daughter. Shall I give two thirds of my wealth away in charity?" He said, "No." I said, "Shall I then give one half of it in charity?"

He said, "No. One third, yet one third is much. It is better to leave your children wealthy than to leave them poor, reduced to begging from others."

The wording is from Sahih Muslim.

الحديث الأربعون

أجمع العلماء على أن من له وارث

لا تنفذ وصيته بزيادة على الثلث إلا بإجازته

روى البخاري ومسلم عن سعد بن أبي وقاص:

قَالَ عَادَنِي رَسُولُ اللَّهِ ﷺ فِي حَجَّةِ الْوَدَاعِ مِنْ وَجَعٍ أَشْفَيْتُ مِنْهُ عَلَى الْمَوْتِ

فَقُلْتُ يَا رَسُولَ اللَّهِ ، بَلَغَنِي مَا تَرَى مِنَ الْوَجَعِ وَأَنَا ذُو مَالٍ وَلاَ يَرِثُنِي إِلاَّ ابْنَةٌ لِي

وَاحِدَةٌ ، أَفَأَتَصَدَّقُ بِثُلُثَيْ مَالِي؟ قَالَ « لاَ ». قَالَ قُلْتُ أَفَأَتَصَدَّقُ بِشَطْرِهِ ؟

قَالَ « لاَ ، الثُّلُثُ وَالثُّلُثُ كَثِيرٌ إِنَّكَ أَنْ تَذَرَ وَرَثَتَكَ أَغْنِيَاءَ خَيْرٌ مِنْ أَنْ تَذَرَهُمْ

عَالَةً يَتَكَفَّفُونَ النَّاسَ.»

واللفظ لمسلم.

Hadith 41

The Most High's statement: Your fathers and your brothers, you do no know which of them will be closest to you in benefit

Al-Bukhārī and Muslim collect from Ibn ʿAbbās that Allah's messenger ﷺ said:

"Grant the inheritance portions to their recipients; whatever remains goes to the closest male relative."

الحديث الحادي الأربعون

قوله تعالى : آبَاؤُكُمْ وَأَبْنَاؤُكُمْ لَا تَدْرُونَ أَيُّهُمْ أَقْرَبُ لَكُمْ نَفْعًا...الآية

روى البخاري ومسلم عَنِ ابْنِ عَبَّاسٍ ، رَضِيَ اللَّهُ عَنْهُمَا ، عَنِ النبي ﷺ قَالَ :

« أَلْحِقُوا الْفَرَائِضَ بِأَهْلِهَا فَمَا بَقِيَ فَلِأَوْلَى رَجُلٍ ذَكَرٍ . »

Hadith 42

The Most High's statement: Commanded of you, when any of you if visited by death while leaving behind some good, is to write a will.

Al-Bukhārī and Muslim collect from Ibn 'Umar that Allah's messenger ﷺ said:

"It is unbefitting of a Muslim who has something which is to be given as a bequest to sleep for three nights without having his will written down regarding it." Abdullah b. Umar said: Since I heard this from Allah's messenger ﷺ, I have not slept for even one night except that my will was with me.

This is the wording of Muslim. In al-Bukhari "…. sleep for two nights…"

الحديث الثاني والأربعون

قوله تعالى: كُتِبَ عَلَيْكُمْ إِذَا حَضَرَ أَحَدَكُمُ الْمَوْتُ
إِنْ تَرَكَ خَيْرًا الْوَصِيَّةُ ...الآية

روى البخاري ومسلم عَنْ ابْنِ عُمَرَ ، رَضِيَ اللَّهُ عَنْهُمَا أَنَّ رَسُولَ اللهِ ﷺ قَالَ :

« مَا حَقُّ امْرِئٍ مُسْلِمٍ لَهُ شَيْءٌ يُوصِي فِيهِ يَبِيتُ ثَلَاثَ لَيَالٍ إِلاَّ وَوَصِيَّتُهُ مَكْتُوبَةٌ
عِنْدَهُ.» قال عبد الله بن عمر ما مرت على ليلة منذ سمعت رسول الله ﷺ قال
ذلك إلا وعندى وصيتى.

هذا اللفظ لمسلم ، وعند البخاري (...يَبِيتُ لَيْلَتَيْنِ...).

The end.

All Praise is due to Allah

through Whose blessings good is completed

and May He sanctify our Prophet Muhammad,

his family and his companions,

all together.

تمّت

والحمد لله

الذي بنعمته تتم الصالحات ،

وصلى الله على نبينا محمد

وعلى آله وأصحابه

أجمعين.

Printed in the USA
CPSIA information can be obtained
at www.ICGtesting.com
LVHW041457090923
757264LV00006B/1324